"I believe in tracts. As a child, I went with my parents and friends from our church to help pass out tracts. Response to evangelical activity in Latin America in those days was often quite negative, but the Lord used those tracts to plant the seed of the gospel in many hearts—including my own. Tracts still work today. My evangelistic team frequently receives letters from people reached for Jesus Christ through the witness of tracts. We're glad to be co-laborers with the American Tract Society, which has assisted our team immeasurably as we've ministered around the world."

Luis Palau, International Evangelist
Luis Palau Evangelistic Association

"The American Tract Society has been the standard in gospel tracts for over 180 years. I endorse ATS because of their ability to get the gospel message out in ways that continually reach the ever-changing world. ATS tracts are one of the best ways to share the simple message of Jesus Christ."

Greg Laurie, Pastor & Evangelist
Harvest Ministries

"Christians everywhere desire to share the gospel with their friends, relatives, neighbors, colleagues and even strangers, when appropriate. Most, however, don't know how to go about such a daunting task. They need training. *Fast Food Evangelism* fits the bill. What boot camp is to a new soldier, *Fast Food Evangelism* is to the believer. It is a crash course in effective evangelistic methods. While it does not replace a traditional Bible college or seminary course in personal evangelism, it provides practical advice and tools for any believer who wishes to join in the Great Commission. I highly recommend it!"

R. Alan Streett, Ph.D., Chair, Evangelism and Pastoral Ministry
Criswell College, Dallas, Texas

"For over 180 years, the American Tract Society has produced some of the finest tracts available. We are delighted to endorse this great ministry. I've discovered through the years that apart from personal, one-on-one witnessing, a tract is the best possible way to communicate the gospel."

Bill Bright, Founder (deceased)
Campus Crusade for Christ

"From time to time God raises up people, agencies, or ministries that result in literally thousands upon thousands of people coming to know Jesus Christ. The American Tract Society is one of those agencies that God has used and continues to use in the advancement of Christ's kingdom here on earth."

Rev. Thomas E. Trask, General Superintendent
Assemblies of God

FAST FOOD
EVANGELISM

*A Drive-Through Approach to
Sharing Christ*

American Tract Society

Written by David LeFlore

Edited by Peter Batzing

Bridge-Logos
Orlando, Florida 32822

Bridge-Logos

Orlando, FL 32822 USA

Fast Food Evangelism
Written by David LeFlore
Edited by Peter Batzing

Copyright ©2007 by Bridge-Logos

Printed in the United States of America.

Library of Congress Catalog Card Number: 2006940989
International Standard Book Number 978-0-88270-341-1

Cover design by Dan Thompson
Chapter 9 by Lindsay Terry
"20 Ways to Use Tracts" by Daniel Southern

Contents

FOREWORD

In the last few decades, the church has heard so much, read so often, and been so strongly encouraged to engage in relational evangelism that some have come to believe that this is the only way evangelism can be done. Thus there is a great need for a book like *Fast Food Evangelism.*

The book is a practical guide to a spontaneous type of evangelism that centers on the use of tracts. Just as there is an innate physical hunger in people, so do people have a hunger for spiritual things. Reminding the reader that most evangelism in the New Testament is not relational but more akin to the fast-food variety, this relatively short book covers most of the salient points a book on evangelism should cover.

The reader will find here a book on evangelism written by one who is a practitioner and not merely a theoretician. He writes briefly, but knowledgeably, about the Holy Spirit, prayer, Scripture memory, and personal testimony as those relate to evangelism.

This is a very practical book. There are study sections, helps in Scripture memory, and above all, great suggestions for the use of tracts in *Fast Food Evangelism.*

Roy J. Fish, Distinguished Professor of Evangelism
Southwestern Baptist Theological Seminary

Fast-Food Evangelism

A Drive-Through Approach to Sharing Christ

Everywhere we look, people are in a hurry. From our internet connections to microwave dinners to the way we drive our cars ... so many aspects of our lives involve some sort of streamlining. We want to cut corners, cut costs, and cut time. And nowhere in our country is this more readily evident than in how and where we eat our food.

Each day in America, over 46 million people eat something from a fast-food restaurant. In 2005 we spent over $110 billion doing it. Some studies claim that too much fast food is bad for our health, but other studies that include reasonable dietary guidelines say that a fast-food diet can be quite healthy.

The thing is, people need to eat ... but with busy lives and limited budgets, they find it difficult to do nutritiously. Most do not have the time to prepare good meals at home all the time, or the resources to go out to nice restaurants. That's where fast food comes in. It's quick, inexpensive, and with a little work it can be good for you too.

What Is Fast-Food Evangelism?

In this study we want to give you another way of looking at evangelism. People need Christ, plain and simple. In the last decade or so someone coined the term "friendship evangelism." Spend lots of time with a person. Get to know them. Let them get to know you. Invite them to church.

Friendship evangelism is a great concept, but unfortunately most of us don't practice it for many of the same reasons we don't eat every meal at a nice restaurant; we don't have the time, energy or resources to do it. That's where Fast-Food Evangelism comes in.

Fast-Food Evangelism shows us that everyone has the time and ability needed to do a great job of sharing Christ. Fast-Food Evangelism doesn't take a lot of time, cost a lot of money, or require a complete lifestyle change. Sure, it's still nice to eat at that nice restaurant on occasion, but for everyday living, fast food is the way to go.

But before we get into the "how to" of Fast-Food Evangelism, let's talk about "why?" Why would we want to share Christ? Why *should* we want to? And how do gospel tracts fit into the planning?

To get our hearts right for sharing the gospel, the first steps are developing a God-given burden for lost people and a genuine appreciation for the aid of gospel tracts in doing that.

Why Evangelize?

Most of us are not "evangelists" according to the classic definition. We reserve that role for the Billy Grahams or talented preachers of our day. But the Bible is clear that *we* are to share the gospel.

Why Us?
God has chosen to reach the world through us. In fact, God uses our faithful (and sometimes fearful) efforts at evangelism to grow us. Through evangelizing we must commit ourselves to God in trust and we must be familiar with His Word. The more we know about God, the better our ability to answer the questions put before us.

There are many other blessings associated with evangelizing, but the greatest is the personal joy of seeing someone come into a relationship with Christ. And of course, one of the most effective methods of evangelizing available is the distribution of quality gospel tracts.

Why Tracts?
It has been said that nothing costs less, goes farther, lasts longer, or says it better than a gospel tract. But what is a tract? In short, a tract is any tool that is to the point, relevant, arrests our attention, contains the gospel, and takes us closer to Christ. At the American Tract Society we have been developing these tools for over 180 years.

Tracts are indispensable. You need to think about their strategic use as you go out into the world each day. When you make them part of your spiritual repertoire, God will give you many opportunities to share. A good tract is so wonderfully crafted that it can go to work if even a child finds it on the floor. Regardless of your spiritual maturity or experience in sharing the gospel, a tract is an indispensable helper.

Fast-Food Evangelism is much like running a fast-food restaurant. There are some basic principles you need to know and put into action in order to be successful. This is the heart of our study.

LESSON 1

People Are Hungry

People Need Christ

The essence of making any business succeed, including a fast-food restaurant, is the ability to see the needs of other people. If your stomach is full you may not think about food. But if you consider the fact that other people are still hungry, you'll see their need, and a great opportunity.

It's the same with our faith. We are born-again believers in Jesus Christ, so we are not generally searching for Him anymore. But what about those who don't yet know Him? How often do we consider them? Just like with running a restaurant, if we think about other people who are lost without Christ, we will see their need, and a tremendous opportunity.

KEY VERSES: (write out the main point of each verse reference)

Philemon 1:6—*I pray that you may be active in sharing your faith, so that you will have a full understanding of every good thing we have in Christ.*

_____

_____

_____

_____

_____

_____

_____

Mark 6:34—*When Jesus landed and saw a large crowd, he had compassion on them, because they were like sheep without a shepherd. So he began teaching them many things.*

_____

_____

_____

_____

_____

_____

_____

_____

John 13:1—[Jesus Washes His Disciples' Feet] *It was just before the Passover Feast. Jesus knew that the time had come for him to leave this world and go to the Father. Having loved his own who were in the world, he now showed them the full extent of his love.*

---

1 John 3:16—*This is how we know what love is: Jesus Christ laid down his life for us. And we ought to lay down our lives for our brothers.*

Jesus tells us in Matthew 28 to "go and make disciples" (v. 19). If we take a closer look at the word "disciple," we find that it simply means "a learner or student" of a particular subject. Mimi is a "disciple" of the Dallas Cowboys. She can tell you who plays at each position, their weight, height and how fast they run the 40 yard dash. Mimi has spent many hours reading about and studying the Cowboy's roster. She is, because of her love for the Cowboys, a "disciple" of the Dallas Cowboys.

Jesus has called each believer to be His disciple, or follower. If we are going to evangelize the way that our Master taught, we must learn and study His methods. The first thing we notice from the Gospels is that Jesus had a heart for the lost. Jesus made this well-known statement in Luke 19:10, *"For the Son of Man came to seek and to save that which was lost" (NKJV).*

Jesus also had a special place in His heart for lost children. Teaching His disciples one day He used a group of little children nearby to make His point, Jesus stated, *"Your Father in heaven is not willing that any of these little ones should be lost"* (Matthew 18:14). Jesus also used the illustration of a lost sheep, a lost coin, and a lost son to illustrate the importance of His mission and the joy of fulfilling it. *"'This son of mine was dead and is alive again; he was lost and is found.' So they began to celebrate"* (Luke 15:24).

Developing a heart for the lost does not come without prayer and Bible study. It is imperative as Christians that we learn the Word of God. Bible study is a key aspect of our growth as a believer, *BUT* … God can still use you *now*. The question is, "Will you let Him?"

From the moment you realized you were a sinner and received Christ as your Savior, He gave you everything you needed to tell others. As 2 Peter 1:3 tells us, "*His divine power has given us everything we need for life and godliness through our knowledge of him who called us by his own glory and goodness.*" Did you see that? His power has given you **all you need** to live a godly life.

Isn't it encouraging to know that our Lord has already made the way for us? Jesus didn't tell us in Matthew 28 to "go study the Bible," although we should. Jesus told us to "*go and make disciples,*" and He gave us everything we need to do so.

Know the Menu

Memorizing Scripture

No one opens a business or restaurant without knowing every one of their products. When you enter a fast-food restaurant, have you ever noticed that your "server" behind the counter is facing you, not the menu overhead? That's because they have it memorized. They know it inside and out and stand ready to help you understand it.

The same should hold true as we attempt to "serve" Christ to people. They will ask questions seeking our help and guidance. This process is so much less stressful, and more effective, when we have the basic salvation Scriptures committed to memory.

KEY VERSES

Deuteronomy 11:18—*Fix these words of mine in your hearts and minds; tie them as symbols on your hands and bind them on your foreheads.*

_____

_____

_____

_____

_____

_____

_____

_____

_____

Psalm 119:11—*I have hidden your word in my heart that I might not sin against you.*

_____

_____

_____

_____

_____

_____

_____

_____

_____

Luke 8:15— *The seed on good soil stands for those with a noble and good heart, who hear the word, retain it, and by persevering produce a crop.*

_____

_____

_____

_____

_____

_____

_____

_____

_____

Romans 10:8— *What does it say? "The word is near you; it is in your mouth and in your heart," that is, the word of faith we are proclaiming.*

_____

_____

_____

_____

_____

_____

_____

_____

_____

Colossians 3:16—*Let the word of Christ dwell in you richly as you teach and admonish one another with all wisdom, and as you sing psalms, hymns and spiritual songs with gratitude in your hearts to God.*

_____

_____

_____

_____

_____

_____

_____

_____

You might be wondering, "How can God use me if I don't have all the right Scripture memorized?" Luke gives us the answer in Acts 1:8, *"You will receive power when the Holy Spirit comes on you; and you will be my witnesses ... ."* Jesus tells us to evangelize now! The moment you become a Christian you have all you need to be used by God ... the Holy Spirit. Isn't that exciting? You don't need anything else ... school, church, the pastor, or anything else. The Holy Spirit has prepared you for witnessing. OK, so why are you spending the time to take this course? To be better equipped to share the love of Christ.

The same holds true as a new believer or any believer who has yet to commit to regular Bible study. To be fully used by God we must be fully prepared. The writer of Hebrews tells us, *"For the word of God is living and active. Sharper than any double-*

edged sword, it penetrates even to dividing soul and spirit, joints and marrow; it judges the thoughts and attitudes of the heart. Nothing in all creation is hidden from God's sight. Everything is uncovered and laid bare before the eyes of him to whom we must give account" (Hebrews 4:12,13).

Allow God's Word to be living and active inside you. We need to spend time each day reading the Bible and talking to God. Here are some verses known as the Romans Road. This is a great place to begin memorizing God's Word to be used in evangelism.

Begin Memorizing Scripture

Who is good?
Romans 3:10—*"As it is written: There is no one righteous, not even one."*

Who has sinned?
Romans 3:23—*"All have sinned and fall short of the glory of God."*

Where sin came from.
Romans 5:12—*"Therefore, just as sin entered the world through one man [Adam], and death through sin, and in this way death came to all men, because all sinned."*

God's price for sin.
Romans 6:23—*"The wages of sin is death, but the gift of God is eternal life in Christ Jesus our Lord."*

Who paid the price?
Romans 5:8—*"But God demonstrates his own love for us in this: While we were still sinners, Christ died for us."*

The only way out.
Romans 10:9, 10—"*That if you confess with your mouth, "Jesus is Lord," and believe in your heart that God raised him from the dead, you will be saved. For it is with your heart that you believe and are justified, and it is with your mouth that you confess and are saved.*"

Claim God's promise for your salvation.
Romans 10:13 —"*Everyone who calls on the name of the Lord will be saved.*"

The Romans Road gives us a great starting point for learning and incorporating Scripture into our witnessing opportunities. To effectively witness to someone about the Good News of Jesus, it is imperative that we study the Master and ask Him to give us a heart for the lost.

Be Ready for the Customer

The Importance of Prayer

Restaurant employees always report to work long before the first customer comes through the door. They turn on the lights, clean the tables and floors, and get things started in the kitchen. The food items have been decided, ordered, shipped, and are often already starting to cook. After all, it would not be much of a restaurant if nothing was ready when the hungry customer showed up.

Fast-Food Evangelism is much the same. Nothing can happen without the purposed preparation of prayer. Prayer that you as the presenter will have the right words to say. Prayer that your "customer's" heart will be ready to receive God's truth. Prayer that the Lord will take charge of the situation and illuminate Himself to the person you talk to or the one who reads your tract.

KEY VERSES

Matthew 6:6 — *But when you pray, go into your room, close the door and pray to your Father, who is unseen. Then your Father, who sees what is done in secret, will reward you.*

_____

_____

_____

_____

_____

_____

_____

Colossians 1:9, 10 — *For this reason, since the day we heard about you, we have not stopped praying for you and asking God to fill you with the knowledge of his will through all spiritual wisdom and understanding. And we pray this in order that you may live a life worthy of the Lord and may please him in every way: bearing fruit in every good work, growing in the knowledge of God ...*

_____

_____

_____

_____

_____

_____

1 Thessalonians 5:16-18—*Be joyful always; pray continually; give thanks in all circumstances, for this is God's will for you in Christ Jesus.*

_____

_____

_____

_____

_____

_____

_____

_____

_____

Mark 6:45, 46—*Immediately Jesus made his disciples get into the boat and go on ahead of him to Bethsaida, while he dismissed the crowd. After leaving them, he went up on a mountainside to pray.*

_____

_____

_____

_____

_____

_____

_____

_____

_____

_____

Romans 10:1—*Brothers, my heart's desire and prayer to God for the Israelites is that they may be saved.*

In a survey taken by Barna Research 2005, we see the effect of prayer on pastors.

The most frequently mentioned priorities of 614 Senior Pastors were discipleship and spiritual development (47%); evangelism and outreach (46%); and preaching (35%).

The second level of priorities included congregational care efforts, such as visitation and counseling (24%); worship (19%); ministry to teenagers and young adults (17%); missions (15%); community service (15%); ministry to children (13%); and congregational fellowship (11%).

The lowest priorities among the dozen ministries described by pastors were ministry to families (4%) **and prayer** (3%).

Did you catch that? Forty-six percent of the pastors surveyed mentioned evangelism and outreach as a major focus for their churches, but only three percent of those same pastors thought that prayer should be a major focus in their churches. The great pastor and preacher of yesteryear, Charles H. Spurgeon said, "Winners of souls must first be weepers of souls."

Jesus Himself knew the importance of prayer. Jesus' first recorded prayer for Himself occurs in John 17:1-5. In verse 3, He said, *"Now this is eternal life: that they may know you, the only true God, and Jesus Christ, whom you have sent."* Further down in verses 6-19, Jesus prayed for His disciples. Jesus said, *"As you sent me into the world, I have sent them into the world."* And in verses 20-26, Jesus prayed for you and me, *"I pray also for those who will believe in me through their message, that all of them may be one."* Jesus completely understood the power of prayer. If prayer was not important, why would Jesus pray for all the believers that would follow His death, burial, and resurrection?

Read John 17 in its entirety. Take a minute to pray for someone you know.

The apostle Paul also knew the importance of prayer. In his letter to the believers in Colossae he wrote, *"We have not stopped praying for you and asking God to fill you with the knowledge of his will through all spiritual wisdom and understanding. And we pray this in order that you may live a life worthy of the Lord and may please him in every way: bearing fruit in every good work, growing in the knowledge of God"* (Colossians 1:9, 10).

In his book *How To Share Your Faith*, pastor and evangelist Greg Laurie writes, "There is a time to pray and a time to move—a time to sow and a time to reap. But it all starts with a God-given burden for lost people." How do we get this "God-given burden?" With prayer! It is essential for believers to get on their knees in front of God's throne and ask for His heart and His burden for the lost. Without prayer we will not be prepared to share the gospel with anyone. It is through prayer that we meet the Holy Spirit face to face and begin to understand His calling to us for reaching the world for Christ. In prayer we can confess our sins, give thanks, ask for His blessings on others, and pray specifically for those with whom we come in contact.

Make a list here of lost people God has put on your heart to pray for.

_____

_____

_____

_____

_____

_____

_____

_____

_____

Prayer Evangelism

A relatively new concept is called "Prayer Evangelism." Prayer evangelism, simply put, is praying for those whom we meet on a daily basis, by name. If you are going to the dentist, doctor, bank or grocery store, pray specifically for those that you will see. "Father, as I go to the store today give me an opportunity to share Your love with the person that is working the register." It is getting down to the grassroots of evangelism. We must pray for opportunities to witness and for those to whom we will be witnessing.

If evangelism is "fishing," then prayer evangelism is like "casting a chartreuse Willywonka # 10 three feet from that log and letting it drop six inches before reeling it in with a counter rotational bobbing motion." Although it doesn't take the place of witnessing, prayer is a very specific and aggressive form of evangelism. You aggressively pray for a specific person before you witness to them. Ask God to prepare their heart, and for the circumstances and opportunity to share the gospel with them. If you want to share the gospel with your family member, friend or neighbor, pray for them by name before you go charging in with your Bible open and wielding the cross as if it were a sword. Get on your knees and pray.

The Four Food Groups

A Balanced Approach

The food we eat has been categorized into four main groups in order to help us better understand nutrition. Grain products, vegetables and fruit, milk products, and meat and alternatives all make up a "balanced" diet.

It's no different with the basics of the gospel. The Romans Road we examined in lesson number two is one way to organize the key theological points of salvation into an easy-to-remember presentation. Here we present another, a four-part process developed by Billy Graham called "Steps to Peace With God." Familiarizing yourself with each of these steps and "balancing" them into a cohesive presentation will go a long way to helping your hearer understand the gospel.

KEY VERSES

John 3:16-17—*For God so loved the world that he gave his one and only Son, that whoever believes in him shall not perish but have eternal life. For God did not send his Son into the world to condemn the world, but to save the world through him.*

_____

_____

_____

_____

_____

_____

_____

_____

1 Corinthians 15:3-5—*For what I received I passed on to you as of first importance: that Christ died for our sins according to the Scriptures, that he was buried, that he was raised on the third day according to the Scriptures, and that he appeared to Peter, and then to the Twelve.*

_____

_____

_____

_____

_____

_____

_____

_____

1 Peter 3:18—*For Christ died for sins once for all, the righteous for the unrighteous, to bring you to God. He was put to death in the body but made alive by the Spirit ...*

_____

_____

_____

_____

_____

_____

_____

_____

The beginning steps of sharing the gospel start with knowing the biblical definition of the word "gospel." If you are going to tell people how to get to heaven, you must know what the "gospel" is.

In 1 Corinthians 15:3-5, we see a clear explanation. *"For I delivered to you first of all that which I also received: that Christ died for our sins according to the Scriptures, and that He was buried, and that He rose again the third day according to the Scriptures, and that He was seen by Cephas, then by the twelve"* (NKJV).

The Reverend Billy Graham has explained this in **four basic steps** that a non-believer should progressively understand. It will help in your own presentation if you know the general flow of Mr. Graham's argument. (This is where a tract comes in handy ... this whole dialogue can be right in front of you.)

23

STEPS TO PEACE WITH GOD
by Billy Graham

Step 1—GOD'S PURPOSE: Peace and Eternal Life
God loves you, and He wants you to live in peace with Him and to receive eternal life.

The Bible Says:
"... we have peace with God through our Lord Jesus Christ" (Romans 5:1b).

"For God so loved the world that He gave His only begotten Son, that whoever believes in Him should not perish but have everlasting life" (John 3:16 NKJV).

"... the gift of God is eternal life in Christ Jesus our Lord" (Romans 6:23b).

Since God planned for us to be at peace with Him and to have eternal life, why are many people not enjoying this experience?

Step 2—OUR PROBLEM: Sin and Separation
God did not make us robots to mindlessly love and obey Him. Instead He gave us a will and freedom of choice. But, like Adam, we often choose to disobey God and go our own selfish ways (read Genesis chapters 2-3). This side of our nature is called sin, and it separates us from God.

The Bible Says:
"For all have sinned and fall short of the glory of God ... the wages of sin is death" (Romans 3:23; 6:23).

"So [after Adam sinned] the LORD God banished him from the Garden of Eden ...." (Genesis 3:23a).

"But your iniquities have separated you from your God; [and] your sins have hidden his face from you, so that he will not hear" (Isaiah 59:2).

Our sin separates us from God.

Step 3—GOD'S REMEDY: The Cross
Jesus Christ is the only answer to this problem of separation from God. He died on the cross and rose from the grave to pay the penalty for our sin—completely bridging the gap between us and God.

The Bible Says:
"But God demonstrates his own love for us in this: While we were still sinners, Christ died for us" (Romans 5:8).

"Salvation is found in no one else, for there is no other name under heaven given to men by which we must be saved" (Acts 4:12).

"… God is on one side and all the people on the other side, and Christ Jesus, Himself man, is between them to bring them together …" (1 Timothy 2:5 TLB).

"I tell you the truth, whoever hears my word [Jesus] and believes him who sent me has eternal life and will not be condemned; he has crossed over from death to life" (John 5:2).

God has provided the only way … and we must make the choice …

Step 4—OUR RESPONSE: Receive Christ
We can receive Jesus Christ when we believe in His message and trust in Him alone to save us.

[Jesus said] *Do not let your hearts be troubled. Trust in God; trust also in me"* (John 14:1).

"All the prophets testify about him that everyone who believes in him [Jesus Christ] *receives forgiveness of sins through his name"* (Acts 10:43).

"Yet to all who received him, to those who believed in his name, he gave the right to become children of God" (John 1:12).

HOW TO RECEIVE CHRIST

1. Admit your need (*I am a sinner*).
2. Be willing to turn from your sins (*repent*).
3. Believe that Jesus Christ died for you on the cross and rose from the grave.
4. Through prayer, invite Jesus Christ to come in and control your life through the Holy Spirit. (*Receive Him as your Savior*).

WHAT TO PRAY:
Dear Lord Jesus, I know that I am sinful and I need Your forgiveness. I believe that You died to pay the penalty for my sin. I want to turn from my sin nature and follow You instead. I invite You to come into my heart and life. In Jesus' name. Amen.

GOD'S ASSURANCE: His Word
If you sincerely prayed this prayer and asked Jesus Christ to come into your life, do you know what He has given you?

YOUR NEW LIFE:
When you receive Christ, you are born into God's family through the supernatural work of the Holy Spirit, who indwells

every believer. This is called regeneration or "new birth." God bless you as you begin your wonderful new life in Christ.

The Bible Says ...
" Everyone who calls on the name of the Lord will be saved" (Romans 10:13).

"Neither height nor depth, nor anything else in all creation, will be able to separate us from the love of God that is in Christ Jesus our Lord" (Romans 8:39).

" Therefore, since we have been justified through faith, we have **peace with God** *through our Lord Jesus Christ"* (Romans 5:1).

"He who has the Son has life; he who does not have the Son of God does not have life. These things I have written to you who believe in the name of the Son of God, that you may know that you have eternal life ...." (1 John 5:12, 13 NKJV).

We must be committed to backing up our statements with the facts of the Bible while we witness. But often we can effectively share the gospel to the lost by using only our own story.

LESSON 5

It Pays to Advertise

Telling Your Story

One of the hallmarks of the fast-food industry is their advertising. It's everywhere. TV, magazines, billboards, and direct mail are all effective ways they use to get their message in front of customers. Some of the most effective ads utilize personal stories ... happy customers telling viewers just how wonderful that particular restaurant is.

Why should it be any different with presenting the gospel? Now people can hear all the theory expressed by a real-life example—you! Nothing is more powerful or more convincing than telling someone the story of what Christ has actually done in your life.

KEY VERSES

Psalm 78:4 — *We will not hide them from their children; we will tell the next generation the praiseworthy deeds of the LORD, his power, and the wonders he has done.*

_____

_____

_____

_____

_____

_____

_____

Joel 1:3 — *Tell it to your children, and let your children tell it to their children, and their children to the next generation.*

_____

_____

_____

_____

_____

_____

_____

John 3:21—*Whoever lives by the truth comes into the light, so that it may be seen plainly that what he has done has been done through God."*

_____

_____

_____

_____

_____

_____

_____

_____

So, now that we know exactly what the gospel is—Christ died for our sins and was raised from the dead—we can more clearly witness to those around us. Let's put a little different spin on the phrase, "sharing your faith." Instead of telling people what you *believe*, tell people what you *know*—your story, or testimony. Every believer has a testimony. It is the best starting point for a Christian to tell someone about Jesus and His saving grace. The great thing about telling your testimony is that every believer has one and everyone's testimony is different. The person may have had the gospel presented to them and even heard someone's testimony, but they haven't heard yours. Take some time and put your testimony into a one-minute commercial. One word of advice; when talking to a non-Christian, it's best to use terms they can understand, like "story" as opposed to the Christian-ese "testimony."

If you have ever been in sales or have known someone in sales, you know that they probably had a quick thirty-second to one-minute commercial for the company or product they represented. Telling others the Good News of Jesus' atonement for our sins is not much different.

Remember, your story shouldn't be too long. Take a moment and begin your one-minute story.

_____

_____

_____

_____

_____

_____

_____

_____

_____

_____

_____

_____

Also, your story should relate to the person with whom you are sharing. To do this, you might want to think about having three or four one-minute commercials. Think about the last time you bought something from a salesperson. You could have bought that product or service from many different companies. Why did you buy that particular product from that person or company? Maybe it was because of price or convenience. But more times than not, we buy from people we like and trust. We are reasonably convinced that we need their product, and that it will work for us.

William Barclay wrote, "*There is little use telling people that Christ will bring them joy and peace and power, if our own lives are gloomy, worried and defeated. Men will be persuaded to try the experiment only when they see that for us it has ended in an experience which is much to be desired.*"

We should remember that we need to be likeable, and not confrontational or argumentative, when we are sharing Christ. What is the single most interesting subject people like to talk about? Themselves! Before sharing your story with anyone, learn more about the other person. Find out what makes them tick. What's important to them? What circumstance or action brought you to this time of sharing? Where are they hurting right now? In order for us to be effective communicators for Christ, we must model Christ's communication model.

Now take time to write two more "uniquely you" commercials.

One: _____

_____

_____

_____

_____

_____

_____

_____

_____

_____

_____

_____

Two: _____

_____

_____

_____

_____

_____

_____

_____

_____

_____

Christ communicated to different people in different ways. When he spoke to Nicodemus, He used terms and analogies that Nicodemus would understand. John 3:1-21 reads, *"Now there was a man of the Pharisees named Nicodemus, a member of the Jewish ruling council ... "* (John 3:1). What did John tell us about Nicodemus? First, Nicodemus was a Pharisee, so he was someone who knew the Scriptures well. Second, he was a member of the Jewish ruling council, so he must have been an educated man with a certain amount of responsibility and influence in his community. So Jesus took a more scholarly approach when He shared the gospel with this man.

Remember to speak of faith in Christ or what the Bible tells us, not feelings, church, denomination or ceremony. Speak from a position of truth, not speculation. Jesus was able to take the truths of the Bible and relate those truths to the people with whom He spoke.

Can you think of an example or situation where you witnessed in a factual way?

_____

_____

_____

_____

_____

_____

_____

_____

_____

_____

Do you remember the story of the woman at the well (John 4:7-26)? John gives us another example of Jesus sharing the gospel with someone in a completely different manner than how He shared the gospel with Nicodemus. In John 4:7 we read, "*When a Samaritan woman came to draw water, Jesus said to her, 'Will you give me a drink?'*" Jesus spoke to her in a way that she could easily understand. Water was then, as it is now, a necessity. Drawing water from the well was something that everyone did on a daily basis. Jesus associated eternal life with water. Jesus took a common, everyday chore and turned it into an opportunity to share the gospel.

Jesus already knew this woman's life's story, but as we follow along with John we see that Jesus had the woman tell Him of her pains. We see her response in verse 9b was, "*You are a Jew and I am a Samaritan woman. How can you ask me for a drink*?" The woman knew she shouldn't be associating with Jesus, because He was Jewish. It was frowned upon in those days for the Samaritans and Jews to even speak to one another. And since she was a woman it was even more unacceptable! Notice Jesus took the time to learn the woman's hurts and pains before He told her that He was the gift of Living Water. Jesus allowed her to discover the gift of Living Water by associating eternal life with something easily understood.

These same opportunities are presented to us every day. The question is, "Will we be ready?" Have you missed an opportunity to share the gospel with a friend, co-worker, neighbor or family member because you were not ready or willing to use the opportunity presented to you?

Can you think of times when you missed an opportunity to share the gospel? What would you do differently if you could go back in time, knowing the person were to die the next day?

Opportunity missed: _____

_____

_____

_____

_____

Different response: _____

_____

_____

_____

Opportunity missed: _____

_____

_____

_____

_____

Different response: _____

_____

_____

_____

_____

Opportunity missed: _____

_____

_____

_____

_____

Different response: _____

_____

_____

_____

_____

Opportunity missed: _____

_____

_____

_____

Different response: _____

_____

_____

_____

_____

We can find example after example of the different situations Jesus used to share the gospel. Jesus is the "Bread of Life," the "Lamb of God," or the "Living Water," depending on the situation. Jesus used whatever means necessary to relate to each audience in a very particular way. Again, if we are to follow Jesus' example of telling the gospel, we must be willing to adapt to the many people with whom we will be sharing. If we are sensitive to the leading of the Holy Spirit, we will know how to most effectively share our stories and share the gospel.

Stick to Nutritional Guidelines

Be Obedient

The four food groups mentioned earlier do us no good if we ignore the recommendations for balancing them in our diets. Nutritional information and dietary advice need to be followed in order to help us gain the most benefit from what we eat. This is especially true for those trying to lose weight, athletes in a training program, or persons with health conditions, who all need to reach specific goals through what they eat.

And so it is with living the Christian life. God has set forth certain guidelines for us to follow in order for us to realize the maximum benefit of our relationship with Him. This obedience to God's direction becomes even more important when we attempt to accomplish specific ministry goals ... like evangelizing.

KEY VERSES

Genesis 22:18b—*All nations on earth will be blessed, because you have obeyed me.*

_____

_____

_____

_____

_____

_____

_____

_____

Jeremiah 7:23—*I gave them this command: Obey me, and I will be your God and you will be my people. Walk in all the ways I command you, that it may go well with you.*

_____

_____

_____

_____

_____

_____

_____

_____

_____

Luke 11:28—*He replied, "Blessed rather are those who hear the word of God and obey it."*

_____

_____

_____

_____

_____

_____

_____

_____

_____

Acts 5:29—*Peter and the other apostles replied: "We must obey God rather than men!"*

_____

_____

_____

_____

_____

_____

_____

_____

_____

_____

1 John 2:5—*But if anyone obeys his word, God's love is truly made complete in him. This is how we know we are in him.*

_____

_____

_____

_____

_____

_____

_____

_____

1 John 5:3-4—*This is love for God: to obey his commands. And his commands are not burdensome, for everyone born of God overcomes the world. This is the victory that has overcome the world, even our faith.*

_____

_____

_____

_____

_____

_____

_____

_____

_____

Right about now you may be asking, *"Why must I share the gospel? Isn't prayer enough? Why can't I just pray for those who are lost?"* You know, it doesn't work that way. In the last chapter of Matthew, in what we call the Great Commission, we see that we are mandated to go and share. Jesus said for each of us to "go." Go to the world with the saving grace of Jesus Christ. Jesus didn't tell us to think about it or have a committee meeting about going, He said, "Go." Not everyone is called to be an evangelist, not everyone is called to be a preacher or teacher. Yet all of us have been called to GO! This is a fact that we cannot dismiss. We are called to "go and make disciples." But our calling doesn't stop at *going*. We are called to *make* disciples. The first step in making disciples is sharing the gospel with whomever God places in our path. Making disciples is all about replacing ourselves within the Kingdom of God.

God wants to reward us. Not with earthly things, necessarily, like money or success, but with treasure in heaven. Isaiah writes in chapter 33 verse 6: *"He will be the sure foundation for your times, a rich store of salvation and wisdom and knowledge; the fear of the Lord is the key to this treasure."* Jesus tells us in Matthew 6:19-21 *"Do not store up for yourselves treasures on earth, where moth and rust destroy, and where thieves break in and steal. But store up for yourselves treasures in heaven, where moth and rust do not destroy, and where thieves do not break in and steal. For where your treasure is, there your heart will be also."* The question is, "Where is *your* treasure?" Do you have a God-given burden for the lost? Do you genuinely want to see people's lives changed so they may spend eternity in heaven?

Most of us would say YES to any of those questions. But sadly, most of us have never shared our beliefs about God with our friends and neighbors, much less witnessed to someone to the point of asking them if they want to place their trust in Christ. Why? The number one thing that holds believers back from sharing their beliefs is ... fear: Fear of rejection. Fear of the unknown. Fear of not having all the answers.

Fear not! Remember what Luke wrote in the book of Acts [explanations added], "*You will receive power when the Holy Spirit comes on you; and you will be my witnesses in Jerusalem* [in your home town], *in all Judea and Samaria* [throughout your county and state], *and to the ends of the earth* [throughout your nation and to the rest of the world]." Now that we understand that we possess the power, through the Holy Spirit, to witness to the lost ... how do we put that power into action?

The Beauty of Fast-Food Evangelism:
Fast, Easy, and Effective

Sharing Christ

Fast food works because it's easy, inexpensive and probably the number one reason is that it just plain tastes good. All the preparation, planning, advertising and cooking come together in that greatest of experiences, sitting down to that chocolate shake, burger and fries. (Oops! Make that a salad.)

Likewise, all your study, memorizing, and prayer finally come to fruition when you see someone come to Christ. That's the high-point for so many Christians, seeing God's kingdom expand right in front of their eyes. Nothing produces so much joy in God's heart and in ours as when we realize that He can use us, with all our deficiencies, to change another life forever.

KEY VERSES

Acts 11:19-21—*Now those who had been scattered by the persecution in connection with Stephen traveled as far as Phoenicia, Cyprus and Antioch, telling the message only to Jews. Some of them, however, men from Cyprus and Cyrene, went to Antioch and began to speak to Greeks also, telling them the good news about the Lord Jesus. The Lord's hand was with them, and a great number of people believed and turned to the Lord.*

---

1 Corinthians 1:17, 18—*For Christ did not send me to baptize, but to preach the gospel—not with words of human wisdom, lest the cross of Christ be emptied of its power. For the message of the cross is foolishness to those who are perishing, but to us who are being saved it is the power of God.*

_____

_____

_____

_____

_____

_____

_____

_____

1 Thessalonians 1:4-6—*For we know, brothers loved by God, that he has chosen you, because our gospel came to you not simply with words, but also with power, with the Holy Spirit and with deep conviction. You know how we lived among you for your sake. You became imitators of us and of the Lord; in spite of severe suffering, you welcomed the message with the joy given by the Holy Spirit.*

_____

_____

_____

_____

_____

_____

_____

_____

_____

John 16:7, 8—*I tell you the truth: It is for your good that I am going away. Unless I go away, the Counselor will not come to you; but if I go, I will send him to you. When he comes, he will convict the world of guilt in regard to sin and righteousness and judgment.*

_____

_____

_____

_____

_____

_____

_____

_____

_____

There are hundreds, if not thousands, of ways to share the gospel with unbelievers—from crusades and evangelistic events to intimately sharing the gospel with family or friends. Our job is to share, not to worry about the results.

This is where the use of TRACTS in your personal witnessing opportunities comes in. Let me explain. Most of us, in this fast-paced world, have at one time or another eaten at a fast-food restaurant. Moms taking kids to soccer, ballet, and baseball practice don't always have the time to cook dinner. Business people rushing from one appointment to the other grab a bite as they're off to make the next big deal. Grandma and Grandpa don't want to heat up the kitchen for their dwindling appetite, so they grab something quick and easy.

Fast-food is not for all of us ... all the time ... but it definitely has its place. When done with just a little care and planning it can be as nutritious as eating anywhere else. It's the same with Fast-Food Evangelism. Jesus never told us we had to become friends with someone before we could share the gospel with them. But by His example He showed us to prepare, to plan, and to treat all people with the love and respect we would show our friends.

The notion of friendship evangelism is good, but how often can we effectively put it into practice? When is the last time you verbally shared the gospel with a lost friend? How many lost friends do you have? We typically spend time with people who are similar to us. If you spend time with people who have the same ideas, values and philosophy as you, you probably don't have many lost friends. We look at Jesus' life and see that there were people in His life with whom He grew very close and intimate. But they were believers! They were not the lost. Anytime you see Jesus encounter a lost person, He shared the gospel, Himself, with that person. Jesus didn't tell the woman at the well or the blind man, "Let's become friends so I can share the good news with you." No, He met them where they were in their circumstance and told them the good news of God's Kingdom.

Fast-Food Evangelism recognizes that we don't always have the time to build a relationship with everyone who needs Christ. The use of tracts can be your answer to evangelism. Tracts can be found that are current, relevant and up-to-date on today's culture and problems. Find a tract that you would want to read. Try to stay away from gimmicks, but choose tracts that would glorify God, tracts that would be easily understood by any reader, without explanation. What better way to share the gospel than in a quick, understandable, easy-to-follow pamphlet?

For nearly 200 years Christians in America have spread the gospel of Jesus Christ using the printed page in the form of gospel tracts. Millions of people are already in heaven as a direct result of these printed pamphlets.

The purpose of this booklet is to show Christians how effective tract ministry can be, and to offer suggestions for developing some simple, low-risk, and effective soul-winning habits into their life.

Scripture tells us: *The fruit of the righteous is a tree of life, and he who wins souls is wise* (Proverbs 11:30). Using tracts can be used in conjunction with any other tool or method for sharing the gospel.

To have a successful tract ministry, you must approach it with resolve and determination, and with a plan—an orderly plan. *Everything should be done in a fitting and orderly way* (1 Corinthians 14:40). Before going into the particulars of a suggested plan, consider the following fascinating story.

Super-Size Me

A Big Success Story

Morgan Spurlock made a documentary film in 2003 called Super-Size Me. The movie chronicles Mr. Spurlock's fast-food diet that lasted for thirty days and almost ruined his health. Conversely, another documentary came out soon after of two people who actually became healthier after dieting on nothing but fast-food. And who is not familiar with "Jared" and his well-known success story with Subway sandwiches?

As we noted earlier, personal stories are very powerful motivators. But so are stories of those "exceptional" others who find great success in their endeavors. These are the stories that need to be told, both to encourage us and to change our lives. Stories the world is dying to hear.

KEY VERSES

Psalm 71:14-16—*But as for me, I will always have hope; I will praise you more and more. My mouth will tell of your righteousness, of your salvation all day long, though I know not its measure. I will come and proclaim your mighty acts, O Sovereign LORD; I will proclaim your righteousness, yours alone.*

_____

_____

_____

_____

_____

_____

_____

_____

_____

Matthew 5:15, 16—*Neither do people light a lamp and put it under a bowl. Instead they put it on its stand, and it gives light to everyone in the house. In the same way, let your light shine before men, that they may see your good deeds and praise your Father in heaven.*

_____

_____

_____

_____

_____

_____

_____

_____

_____

Matthew 25:21—*His master replied, "Well done, good and faithful servant! You have been faithful with a few things; I will put you in charge of many things. Come and share your master's happiness!"*

_____

_____

_____

_____

_____

_____

_____

_____

_____

1 Thessalonians 2:4—*On the contrary, we speak as men approved by God to be entrusted with the gospel. We are not trying to please men but God, who tests our hearts.*

_____

_____

_____

_____

_____

_____

_____

_____

_____

1 Peter 4:11—*If anyone speaks, he should do it as one speaking the very words of God. If anyone serves, he should do it with the strength God provides, so that in all things God may be praised through Jesus Christ. To him be the glory and the power for ever and ever. Amen.*

_____

_____

_____

_____

_____

_____

_____

_____

In the summer of 1953, in the Lansdowne Baptist Church in Bournemouth, England, Pastor Francis Dixon, during a time when members of the congregation could stand and give testimonies, heard the testimony of a sailor who had returned from Australia. While on leave in Sydney, he was approached by a small, white haired man on George Street who asked, "Young man, if you were to die tonight, where would you be, in heaven or in hell?" while handing out a tract. The question left such a deep impression on the heart of the sailor that he sought spiritual help when he returned home to England. Pastor Dixon led this young man, Peter Culver, to Christ.

Not long after that experience, Pastor Dixon heard a similar testimony from another sailor who had an encounter with this same little man on George Street in Sydney. The event led to his salvation experience also. Hearing the testimonies of those sailors made a deep impression on the pastor, an impression that would send him on a life-changing adventure into other countries.

Shortly after hearing the stories from the two sailors, Francis Dixon, accompanied by his wife, left England for a preaching venture in Australia and New Zealand. Deeply fascinated by the coincidence of the two stories of the sailors, and recognizing that he was heading to the land where those events took place, he resolved to investigate the matter further, not knowing that he was to later come face-to-face with this unconventional street evangelist. Why had he chosen to minister in such a fashion? As you and I would want to know, I'm sure he was keenly interested in how many people had been impacted by the ministry of a man who gave out tracts on George Street in Sydney and asked, "If you were to die tonight, where would you be, in heaven or in hell?"

It didn't take long for the answers to start coming. The tour began in Adelaide, Australia where he preached in a large hall one night, relating the stories of the two sailors from England.

The words were not far from his lips when the host of the meetings—who was sitting next to Mrs. Dixon—jumped to his feet and shouted, **"I'm another! I'm another!"** This man's name was Murray Wilkes, who later told them that during World War II this street evangelist had approached him on George Street while he was running to catch a tram. Two weeks later after the encounter, he gave his life to Christ in an army barracks.

Pastor Dixon went on to Perth, Australia, where he again shared the story of the two sailors who had been saved. After his sermon a man approached him and said that he too had become a Christian as a consequence of an encounter with a white haired man on George Street in Sydney. He had so grown in Christ that he began to lead Christian Endeavor for Western Australia.

And so, Francis Dixon reached Sydney determined to meet the man behind these stories. On arrival, he related the stories to a local Christian worker, Alec Gilchrist, and asked if he knew the evangelist on George Street. "I know him well," said Alec. "His name is Frank Jenner. Like me, he works with the armed forces and he is a sailor himself. He worships at one of the Christian Brethren assemblies in Sydney."

Shortly thereafter, Pastor Dixon gained proper directions and made his way to Frank Jenner's home, a humble townhouse. When Pastor Dixon shared his stories with Mr. Jenner, tears welled up in the little man's eyes and he fell to his knees in prayer saying, "O Lord, thank you for tolerating me." After a time of prayer, Jenner said that after speaking to at least ten people a day for the previous sixteen years, this was the first time he had heard of lasting results. He said to his guests, "You know, I never heard that anyone I ever spoke to had gone on for the Lord. Some made professions of salvation when I spoke to them, but I never ever knew any more than that."

The circumstances of World War II—particularly the horrific images of Japan after the atomic bombs—so heightened Jenner's sense of urgency that he felt it necessary to confront others directly about their standing before God. It didn't come easily for Jenner, who struggled to overcome difficulties in his life, health problems as well as spiritual challenges. He was so aware of his weakness that before each encounter on George Street he silently prayed, "I can do all things through Him who gives me strength." He first coined his now famous question, "If you were to die tonight, where would you be, in heaven or in hell?" in 1937, and over the years it has been estimated that he asked it at least 100,000 times.

It is not surprising that his influence extended far beyond Australia. Just a month after meeting Frank Jenner, Pastor Dixon spoke at a Methodist Church in Keswick, England. After the service a man who worked for Mission to Mediterranean Garrisons approached him and said, "I too was challenged by Mr. Jenner and now I am in soul-winning work myself."

Four years later while ministering to missionaries in India, Pastor Dixon found another convert from George Street, Sydney. She had responded to the evangelist's challenge and offered her life for service in India.

Frank Jenner got very quickly to the heart of the issue. He directly challenged people about their standing before God. His simple question is not a formula for us to copy, but his life is a wonderful testimony of how God can use those who remain faithful to Him.

I recently corresponded with a man who lives in Australia, Rev. David Smethurst, asking him about Frank Jenner's tract ministry and remarking to him about the huge expense to give out as many tracts as those he witnessed to. David's reply was, "Yes, Frank Jenner did use tracts, but I haven't a clue what type he used, other than a straight-forward gospel tract. His church, a Brethren Chapel, just off George Street, that has since closed, obviously provided him with literature. Mr. Jenner was desperately concerned about the follow-up of those he was trying to lead to Christ. He took them home for meals and, I believe, sometimes had twenty or more seekers in his home for a meal."

Can you imagine the reward when Frank Jenner went home to be in heaven? No one except a little group of Christians in Sydney knew about Mr. Jenner, but he was known to all in heaven.

The harvest truly is plenteous, but the laborers are few; pray ye therefore the Lord of the harvest that He will send forth laborers into His harvest. (Matthew 9:37-38 KJV)

Getting Ready to Open

Making a Plan

Before opening any restaurant, a prudent owner will make a detailed business plan. He does his homework regarding location, building costs and profit projections. He knows how big the building will be, how much money it will make, and how many customers he can expect. He tries to see every contingency that lays ahead and prepares for them the best he can.

To begin a ministry of sharing Christ with people, the good Fast-Food Evangelist will make plans as well. Besides prayer, memorization, and study, you need to know where, when and how you will be giving out tracts. Things will not always go as planned, but with plans in place you will always have a point to return to regroup and remind yourself of your direction.

KEY VERSES

Psalm 33:11 — *The plans of the LORD stand firm forever, the purposes of his heart through all generations.*

_____

_____

_____

_____

_____

_____

_____

_____

Proverbs 15:22, 16:3 — *Plans fail for lack of counsel, but with many advisers they succeed. Commit to the LORD whatever you do, and your plans will succeed.*

_____

_____

_____

_____

_____

_____

_____

_____

_____

Isaiah 32:8—*But the noble man makes noble plans, and by noble deeds he stands.*

_____

_____

_____

_____

_____

_____

_____

_____

_____

_____

Luke 14:28—*Suppose one of you wants to build a tower. Will he not first sit down and estimate the cost to see if he has enough money to complete it?*

_____

_____

_____

_____

_____

_____

_____

_____

_____

First, plan to make your tract ministry...
PERSONAL

Decide from the very beginning that you will do more than simply agree that a tract ministry is a good thing. Do more, even, than financially support a gospel tract publishing ministry, or encourage your church to put a tract rack in the foyer or vestibule. The ultimate goal of any "ministry" is for you to make it personal. Put some tracts in your pocket or purse, step out into the world and hand them out to people with whom you come in contact.

From Your Hand

The most effective tract distribution is a personal process, passing a tract from your hand into the hand of another individual. Of course, there should be some conversation such as, "May I give you something I think you will enjoy reading?" or "I found this very interesting, may I share it with you?"

Mr. Jenner's approach worked for him, but the same process may not work for you. Handing out tracts on the street, such as he did, requires a special grace and determination.

Hundreds of Different Tracts

There is a multiplicity of tracts that you can use to lead others to the Lord. Research them. Read them. Pray about finding just the right ones that match your areas of interest. Find several that you like and that you can talk briefly to people about when giving the tract to them. It will not be easy the first time, but God will help you and give you the grace to keep on keeping on. Leave the results to Him.

Second, make sure you have a plan.
BE CREATIVE

Plan ahead when giving out tracts. We have discussed some
things you might say when giving out tracts, but let's go a little
further with that thought. Let me suggest that you plan, and
pray, well in advance how you might approach certain
individuals that you want to witness to in this manner.

There are many other effective ways to distribute gospel tracts
apart from personal contact. Many of these can be fun and the
sky is the limit as to the variety of ways you may think of to
get tracts into the hands of spiritually needy people. We will
list a very few here—just enough to get you started. See Lesson
ten for more ideas.

- Put tracts in envelopes when paying bills.
- Put tracts in Christmas cards or birthday and anniversary
greetings.
- Put tracts in magazines at the doctor's office. Let them
protrude at the top.
- Leave a tract in the pay phone booth or in a public
restroom.
- Drop special tracts for children in the trick or treat bags
on Halloween.

Once you get going, you will think of dozens of other places
to strategically place a tract where someone will see it and pick
it up. Sometimes you may discover a place while out shopping
or engaged in some other activity. People have written us about
coming to Christ through tracts found on park benches, bus
seats, gas pumps, store countertops, in restaurant booths, rental
car glove boxes, hotel room drawers and on airplanes. This list
is as endless as God's imagination.

BE COMMITTED

Everything good begins with a commitment. Some may say, "I just don't commit to things." Yes, you do! When you buy a house, you commit to paying the mortgage payments. When you buy a piece of land, you commit to paying the taxes on it. When you have a child, you commit yourself to raise him or her in the admonition of the Lord. Let me repeat, "Everything good begins with a commitment."

A successful evangelism ministry requires more commitment than almost any other ministry. First and foremost it requires faithfulness, but boldness must also come to the front. It is easy to let an opportunity get by when giving out tracts. We don't want people to think that we are strange, or odd, or religious nuts and fanatics. But in order to be faithful to that which God wants us to do, we must be willing, if need be, to be called some of those names. *"In fact, everyone who wants to live a godly life in Christ Jesus will be persecuted"* (2 Timothy 3:12).

BE CONSISTENT

When commitment slacks, we become inconsistent. Commitment and consistency must work hand in hand. As you force consistency, you become more committed. Then and only then does this kind of witnessing become a way of life.

Every effort in the tract ministry is powerful
The "power" aspect of this ministry is God's and God's alone. When we submit ourselves to God and do as He has commanded, then He furnishes the power it takes to insure success. *"All authority in heaven and on earth has been given to me"* (Matthew 28:18).

God also says that His Word will not return void. *"So is my word that goes out from my mouth: It will not return to me empty, but will accomplish what I desire and achieve the purpose for which I sent it"* (Isaiah 55:11).

When we do our very best to be faithful to His cause, then we have every right to leave the results to Him—and Him alone. We couldn't save anyone even if we tried. Just as when you were saved, when others come to Christ it must be by His power.

The people who were saved as a result of the witness by Mr. Jenner on George Street were also saved by the power and the providence of Almighty God. God was at work in the lives of those people who were touched with his tract ministry. When we witness to others, we must also leave the results in God's hands. *"No one can come to me unless the Father who sent me draws him"* (John 6:44).

Giving Tracts to Others Often Opens the Door to WITNESS

Another great example of the power and providence of God is illustrated in the following story which happened in the home of Sumner Wemp, a most faithful, effective Christian in witnessing for Christ. He has given out untold thousands of tracts in his lifetime. Here is the story as Sumner told it in November of 2004.

"A year ago a man came to deliver flowers to my wife, Celeste, from her cousin. I thanked him and gave him a gospel tract. He said, 'I just started teaching a Sunday school class.' Then I felt an urge to ask, 'That's great, but do you know for sure you are going to heaven?' It was unreal. He did not know for sure if he was going to heaven. I had the wonderful joy of telling him that God loved him and that His Son, the Lord Jesus suffered and died for all our sins, paid the debt in full and rose again from the grave. He said, 'I never heard it like that before.' He gladly prayed with me, received the Lord Jesus as his Savior, and was gloriously saved. He thanked me five times and said, 'God sent me to you today.'

"Six months later this same man, James, came to our door with flowers from our daughter in Arizona. Imagine the probability of our cousin and our daughter, a thousand miles apart, sending flowers through the same florist. WOW! James said, 'When I saw these were for you, I could not wait to see you again!' He thanked me again and asked, 'Can I pray for you?' 'I would love for you to,' I replied. You should have heard him. He reached all the way to heaven and really got to God for me. What a blessing!

"Imagine the thrill last Wednesday when I went to the door and there was this same 65-year-old man, James, with flowers again! You should have heard him. He was so full of joy and told me how he was asked to be the head of the men's brotherhood in his church. He told of one blessing after another. I stood there about to shout, seeing what God had done in this man's life. I prayed for him and we wept and hugged each other and he left. I wanted to fall on my knees and thank God for the privilege of leading people to Christ."

Your Own Ideas
This booklet is not an exhaustive study of the possibilities of a successful tract ministry, but its intent is to give you an idea of the importance of such a ministry. You may have many more ideas of your own than are presented in this booklet. If so, make the most of it, and share your ideas and burdens with others.

It is our prayer that you will not wait another day before starting a tract ministry of witnessing to others. In addition, we pray your ministry for the Lord will grow as it spreads to the lives of those who will take up the challenge and become witnesses for Christ also. Will you take the Fast-Food Evangelism challenge?

For the next thirty days, we dare you to share the gospel, your testimony, and a tract with at least one person a day.

Watch God work through your obedience to Him!

Start Now! Write Your Ideas

_____

_____

_____

_____

_____

_____

_____

_____

_____

Your First Customer

Stepping Out

W hen that restaurant door first swings open, how exciting it is when those customers finally walk in the door. Now it's time for everything to come together, and for it all to work seamlessly. The dining room's appearance, the counter greeter, the ease of the transaction and finally the food experience all are critical. And as anyone who has ever worked in a fast-food restaurant knows, there are endless guidelines to follow to make sure that the customer is happy.

In fact this theory is not much different when it comes to Fast-Food Evangelism. There are any number of things to keep in mind when talking to people. Most are just basic human courtesies. But the essential point to remember is that you are not in control. The ultimate impression a person gets from your presentation of Christ or from your tract is ultimately not up to you at all.

KEY VERSES

Matthew 28:16-20—*Then the eleven disciples went to Galilee, to the mountain where Jesus had told them to go. When they saw him, they worshiped him; but some doubted. Then Jesus came to them and said, "All authority in heaven and on earth has been given to me. Therefore go and make disciples of all nations, baptizing them in the name of the Father and of the Son and of the Holy Spirit, and teaching them to obey everything I have commanded you. And surely I am with you always, to the very end of the age."*

_____

_____

_____

_____

_____

_____

_____

_____

_____

Acts 1:8—*But you will receive power when the Holy Spirit comes on you; and you will be my witnesses in Jerusalem, and in all Judea and Samaria, and to the ends of the earth.*

_____

_____

_____

_____

_____

_____

_____

_____

_____

_____

Hebrews 4:12, 13—*For the word of God is living and active. Sharper than any double-edged sword, it penetrates even to dividing soul and spirit, joints and marrow; it judges the thoughts and attitudes of the heart. Nothing in all creation is hidden from God's sight. Everything is uncovered and laid bare before the eyes of him to whom we must give account.*

_____

_____

_____

_____

_____

_____

_____

_____

_____

Isaiah 6:8 — *Then I heard the voice of the Lord saying, "Whom shall I send? And who will go for us?" And I said, "Here am I. Send me!"*

_____

_____

_____

_____

_____

_____

_____

_____

_____

_____

As you Fast-Food Evangelize ...

1. Pray.
You cannot win anyone to Christ, and neither can a tract. Only the Holy Spirit can do that.

2. Give appropriate tracts.
Always carry several different types of tracts with you — so you can match the message to the person.

3. Engage your audience.
This can be done by making eye contact, with a simple smile, asking questions and listening carefully to what is said.

4. Don't force tracts on people.
It is better to distribute a dozen tracts carefully, prayerfully, and judiciously than to hand out a hundred indiscriminately.

5. Use top-quality tracts.
Invest in the best tracts available. You and your Lord will be judged by the equipment you use.

6. Keep your tracts in good condition.
Make sure your tracts are clean and fresh when you hand them out.

7. Use positive tracts.
Our job is not to put others down, but to lift Jesus up by presenting the positive truth of the gospel.

8. Find new ways to use tracts.
Be original. Never leave home without a tract.

9. Get organized.
Place tracts where they will be readily accessible for your use, like in your wallet, briefcase, car, backpack, or purse.

10. Give out a tract each day.
You will be amazed as you see the Lord bless your efforts.

20 WAYS TO SHARE GOSPEL TRACTS

1. With greeting cards
2. When you send a letter or package in the mail
3. In a public restroom
4. On the counter in a store/business
5. On a bus, train, taxi or airplane seat
6. With a bill, letter or card in the mail
7. On Halloween at your front door with delicious candy
8. At your church's Fall Festival, Oktoberfest or Living Christmas Tree
9. At work
10. When you travel
11. As an email attachment
12. When you visit someone who is ill at home, in the hospital or nursing home
13. In a tract display at church or business
14. With your company's invoice
15. During door-to-door visitation
16. On street corners to strangers
17. With relatives during family reunions, holidays, weddings, and funerals
18. With prisoners
19. In your home
20. At your business

Future Expansion

Where to Go from Here

The entire fast-food industry started with just one restaurant. The keys to success have now been copied and repeated thousands of times over. What worked was repeated. What didn't was dropped. The goal was and is still to expand the reach of that business to as many as possible.

Of course our motive for evangelism isn't profit, but souls. But the same principles can be applied. Over time you'll find what works best and repeat it. What doesn't work you'll drop. But the most important principle here is that each one who comes to Christ through your efforts duplicates themselves into another Fast-Food Evangelist. Our goal is to reach the world with the life-changing gospel of Jesus Christ.

KEY VERSES

Exodus 18:19-21—*Listen now to me and I will give you some advice, and may God be with you. You must be the people's representative before God and bring their disputes to him. Teach them the decrees and laws, and show them the way to live and the duties they are to perform. But select capable men from all the people—men who fear God, trustworthy men who hate dishonest gain—and appoint them as officials over thousands, hundreds, fifties and tens.*

_____

_____

_____

_____

_____

_____

_____

_____

_____

_____

Deuteronomy 4:9—*Only be careful, and watch yourselves closely so that you do not forget the things your eyes have seen or let them slip from your heart as long as you live. Teach them to your children and to their children after them.*

_____

_____

_____

_____

_____

_____

_____

_____

_____

_____

_____

_____

2 Timothy 2:1-3— *You then, my son, be strong in the grace that is in Christ Jesus. And the things you have heard me say in the presence of many witnesses entrust to reliable men who will also be qualified to teach others. Endure hardship with us like a good soldier of Christ Jesus.*

_____

_____

_____

_____

_____

_____

_____

_____

_____

_____

_____

So what do you do now? How can you use these tips and ideas in everyday life? Let's go back with a quick recap of each lesson's key idea.

DEVELOPING A HEART FOR EVANGELISM
Some people are gifted from God with a heart and ability for evangelism. Most of us do not have this gift, but by recognizing your specific gifts and practicing them daily, God's truth will become more visible to someone. This is the starting point for sharing the gospel.

MEMORIZING SCRIPTURE
When Jesus faced Satan after fasting and praying for forty days, He answered each of Satan's attacks with Scripture. We too must be ready to answer the attacks we might receive when witnessing. Scripture is our best defense from any attack that might be directed at you when you share the truth of the gospel.

THE IMPORTANCE OF PRAYER
Without a deep, personal relationship with our heavenly Father, any attempt to witness will fall on deaf ears. You cannot save anyone…only God can. A person that is connected to God through an active and vibrant prayer life will not only see the opportunities to witness, but also have the power of the Holy Spirit directing those efforts.

KNOW WHERE TO START
This is crucial in sharing the gospel. Remember, the gospel is not complex or hard to define. Christ died for your sins and has risen from the dead. Acceptance of this FACT can bring anyone into a personal relationship with God Himself. Practice sharing these four steps:
    1. God's purpose is for all men to be saved.

2. The problem preventing that is sin.
3. God's answer to the problem is Christ's death and resurrection.
4. Our response is to believe.

YOUR STORY
Your story is very important in sharing the gospel. Yes, we must pray, memorize Scripture, and know how to share the gospel. Your personal story is the glue that binds all these elements together and makes the message personal to all you witness to. Remember—don't exaggerate—be yourself and be relevant.

BE OBEDIENT
Obey God in all He has called you to do. Be obedient in your giving. Be obedient in your prayer life. Be obedient in studying Scripture. Remember that the examples of Jesus' life are as relevant today as they were two thousand years ago. What better example do we have of someone practicing Fast-Food Evangelism? Be obedient in your witnessing life.

SHARING CHRIST
This can happen in many different ways. Using a gospel tract that you like can help in sharing Christ. Remember to use tracts that are relevant to the situation, easily understood, and above all—clearly relay the gospel message.

MAKING A PLAN
Making and putting into practice a plan is crucial in your growing evangelistic opportunities. Don't be afraid to try new ideas. Just be consistent in practicing evangelism and watch the Kingdom grow.

STEPPING OUT
Putting this information to use can be a bit scary, especially if

you have never considered yourself an evangelist. Don't worry! Christ has called us to share the Good News wherever we are in our spiritual walk.

Take baby steps. Do only what is comfortable for you. Start by finding some favorite tracts to keep with you at all times. Give one tract away each day and watch how God will bless you and give you more opportunities to share.

Once you're comfortable giving away tracts, try going through the tract with at least one person each week. Sit down and read the tract with them. This will help you get over the fear or anxiousness of talking to someone about the gospel.

As you get more comfortable, begin to add your own testimony to the conversation. Continue to use the tract, but add some personal experiences into the conversation. Don't forget to find out who you are talking to. What makes them tick? How did they get to this point in their life? Why did God bring you two together? Be real, honest, and sincere and share what God is doing in your life now.

The more times you share the gospel and your personal testimony, the more comfortable it will become for you. Don't be afraid to be creative and try new ideas. If you have a system that works well for you, go to www.atstracts.org and share it with us. We would love your testimony to encourage others in sharing opportunities.

Here's mine:

My brother and I took our kids to a local fast food restaurant, a typical "all you can eat" pizza buffet. (Yes, by the way, I ate all I could.) There was a teenage girl who came by our table clearing off the used plates piled with pizza crust. The first time she came over to our table I noticed she had several body piercings … in her ears, one in her eyebrow, one in her nose and another one in her tongue. Being the inquisitive person that I am, I asked if it hurt when she got them. We chatted a moment or so, and she went back to cleaning the tables, and I continued to eat all I could. When she left I prayed a quick prayer, "Father, give me just the right words to say." I remembered I had a tract with me that talked about Jesus being pierced for our sins, "Pierced." When she came back the third time, I read the tract with her. Then I asked if there was any reason for her not to ask Jesus to be her Savior. She agreed she needed forgiveness from her sins and in the middle of a fast-food restaurant, we bowed together, and in her own words this precious young woman asked Christ into her life.

If we are truly followers of Jesus Christ, we need to follow His example of evangelism. Jesus didn't become "friends" with someone before sharing the gospel with them. He shared the gospel with everyone He met.

I pray that this book will help and encourage you to share the gospel with everyone you meet. As mentioned before, a tract is an easy way to spread the Good News of our Savior!

His Blessings,

David LeFlore
V.P. Evangelism and Outreach
American Tract Society

LESSON 12

Billions Served

Billions Saved

The big red and yellow sign in front of every McDonald's in the world boldly proclaims the huge number of people who have (theoretically) been happily served by the restaurant. The assumption made is that with all those successes, you will feel more comfortable going in yourself. The testimony of those who have boldly gone before you is undoubtedly very encouraging.

Evangelism is no different. Doing something new always produces anxiety, but looking at the results of those who have gone before you will hopefully be an encouragement.

KEY VERSE

Acts 3:1-10—*One day Peter and John were going up to the temple at the time of prayer—at three in the afternoon. Now a man crippled from birth was being carried to the temple gate called Beautiful, where he was put every day to beg from those going into the temple courts. When he saw Peter and John about to enter, he asked them for money. Peter looked straight at him, as did John. Then Peter said, "Look at us!" So the man gave them his attention, expecting to get something from them.*

Then Peter said, "Silver or gold I do not have, but what I have I give you. In the name of Jesus Christ of Nazareth, walk." Taking him by the right hand, he helped him up, and instantly the man's feet and ankles became strong. He jumped to his feet and began to walk. Then he went with them into the temple courts, walking and jumping, and praising God. When all the people saw him walking and praising God, they recognized him as the same man who used to sit begging at the temple gate called Beautiful, and they were filled with wonder and amazement at what had happened to him.

_____

_____

_____

_____

_____

_____

_____

_____

_____

_____

I got this invitation (tract) while taking my son trick-or-treating. I would like to learn more about our Lord. – Karen

I have really enjoyed your tracts. When I get through with them, I carry them to my job and leave them on the magazine rack, in the bathroom or emergency waiting room. You gave me something, and I pass it on to others. – Anita

My wife received your tract in a doctor's office and gave it to our son Daniel to read. It surprised me a lot that he gave it to his mother to mail (to you). I believe that God touched his heart. – Alfonso

I have trusted Jesus to save me from my sins. My mother sent me a handout, and I really enjoyed it. – Michael

I received this from an anonymous sender. I read it and prayed to receive Jesus as my Savior. – John

I received a Christmas card from my cousin that told the story of the Christmas wreath, and it had a prayer to accept Jesus Christ as my Savior. My husband and I have been talking a lot about Jesus Christ. We're eager to learn about His work and would like to gain wisdom to share. – Christel

I received your tract, Father's Love Letter, from my grandmother. I've given my life back over to the Lord and that helped me out a whole lot. I thank you. God bless you and your ministry! – Michael

Today I have decided to accept God's offer of eternal life through Jesus Christ. A friend sent this tract to me! – Jane, age 82

After church we went to a restaurant to get a bite to eat with

some friends. I went to the bathroom to wash my hands. There were two tracts and I picked one up that said, "You Are Someone Special!" I put it in my purse and walked out. When I got home, I read it and asked God to come into my heart. Thank you so much. – Judy

I got this little booklet when I was at a store right down the road from my home. I picked it up and brought it home. I started reading it and it really touched my heart. – Brittany, age 16

I was really empty inside and my cousin and I went for a bus ride to look for something to satisfy our spirits. I read this tract and I felt like Tom Landry. I now believe in Christ and would please like some information on my walk with Christ. – Salvador

I'm sending you the tract I found on the bus. I have just prayed to receive Christ as my Savior. – Mrs. H

I am thankful to the lady that came into the bank and brought this pamphlet to me. It's good to see people spreading the world of the Lord. – LaTonia

My grandma was a believer and loved the Lord. I never knew how much and how she served Him until her recent death and funeral. Stories were shared about her and the many ways she shared the gospel. One of the ways was with tracts. She used to insert them into her bills she way paying. Hearing stories about her has stirred me to pick up where she left off. I look forward to receiving my order and getting down to business. – Debbie

Today I was opening the mail at work when an insert caught my eye. It was in regards to Thanksgiving and counting our blessings. Something made me stop what I was doing and read the insert as well as log onto the website. After reading some *things here, I have realized I need to take the Lord into my heart and keep him there.* – Elizabeth

All of us prayed this prayer (age 32, 28, and 5). Even my 5 year old! This was a great insight! Thank you! – Robert

Thanks for blessing me with this wonderful gift! – Stephen, age 12

I took my three children to our church on Halloween. When we got home, we went through their bags so see what they got. I found a booklet with Darth Vader on the front, The True Force. I am a big Star Wars fan and my son was Darth Vader for Halloween. That booklet forever changed my life! I read it to my kids and I have read it a number of times alone. I love the Lord and want to serve him each and every day of my life! – Jeff

For the last three years our church has held an outreach event we call Trunk or Treat. Every October 31st, we outline our parking lot with about 100 decorated cars with trunks open and passing out candy. To add to the atmosphere, we have several carnival games, moon bounces, hayrides, outdoor cartoons, concession stands, a fun maze, and live radio show.

We have grown in number since the first year, and this year we had 3,000 on our property for the night. Every one of these years has been blessed with your ministry's participation. Each guest receives a bag with our church information, a few sponsor gifts, and three tracts from your ministry. Thank you for seeing the need to provide a variety for tracts that match seasons, life experiences, ages, and calendar events. We look forward to having you here, in written form, every year! – Roy, Children's Pastor

I have just accepted Jesus. Sorry for the photocopy that I'm sending you, but I enjoyed the story of the candy cane so much that I gave it to one of my co-workers to read and pass on. – Starr

Last week I was surprised when an officer in my jail block started handing out tracts about prayer and faith. I did read the tract on survival on the inside and yes, I've prayed to receive Jesus as my Savior and I have! – Ronald

I just ordered five packs of The Brotherhood *(biker tract). We minister to unsaved bikers, including a lot of outlaws. We give out lots of tracts at bike events and we've been waiting for someone to write a tract about bikers. I just wanted to let you at A.T.S. know that we really like this tract and we've been handing it out in the biker community. Thank you for addressing the biker community. These tracts help us spread the Gospel in some dark places.* – Donna

Wonderful! This tract made me feel so special in God's sight. Through this tract, I was able to discover who I really was. I am sending this to my friends too. Thanks, Digitract! – Wilson (from India, through our website)

Very good website! I want to send this tract to my unbelieving relatives, and they are very computer savvy, so I'm sure they will check you out. Thanks for the good salvation message! – Jean

I work in a nursing home and one of our residents puts these tracts in different places. I'm in housekeeping and was in one of the lounges that doesn't get used much and found this tract. After reading this tract, I have accepted Jesus as my Savior. – Yolanda

We have been using your tracts in our "holy grounds" visitors' area over the last few months. A gentleman left this tract with his name and address after reading and accepting the gift of our Lord, salvation. I wanted to share with you the fruits of your labor. Thank you for all that you do and we are honored to have your materials in our visitor area. May God continue to bless what you do. – Jerry

We discovered the enclosed tract in our tract rack along with the other tracts that we use for our prison ministry. It's a great tract! The little box was checked that read: "I have just prayed to receive Jesus as my Savior." – Michael

Our company has been witnessing for the Lord through business commerce since 1952 and often includes tracts enclosed with our billing and mailings. One of our customers has filled out the back of this tract and sent it to us rather than to A.T.S. We are thrilled to have received this response and ask that you please contact him regarding his decision. – The McNichols Company

I have just asked God, through Christ, to forgive my sins. – Thomas

I really enjoy getting your little booklets in our invoices. They really mean a lot to me and my family! – Marybeth

I was on drugs, almost homeless, angry at the world and didn't care about anyone but myself. I had decided to end my life, and as I stepped out onto my porch for the last time to look up into the heavens and say my farewells, I stepped on something. So I reached down to pick it up and saw it was a tract that said, "Where Will You Spend Eternity?!!" That got me to thinking, and that's when I made up my mind to choose where I will live after I leave this world! And since then, my head has been

89

straight. That tract is a blessing in my life! – Eula

I want to ask Jesus into my life. There's this old lady who comes over to the corner where me and my friends hang out and gives us tracts. She's done that a lot of times. This week she gave us one called Where Will You Spend Eternity? *For some reason I took it home and read it. God spoke to me and I knew I needed to call and get things right with God.* – Josh, age 14,

I have accepted the road of Christ. I've fought it for many years, but I finally see the light. A man and his child gave this pamphlet to me. Thank you, Jesus! – Bobbie

I received one of your pamphlets when I was visiting some family in Garland, TX. I have been hungry for the word of God for some time and think I have finally found my direction. – Ana

I received these tracts through a prison package that was sent to me. I have just received Jesus into my life. – Williams

I saw your pamphlet on the table here in the jail and I guess it was meant for me to read it. – Jeff

Years back, I remember my grandmother having a copy of Power for Living, *but I never once picked it up. But now, I've found myself with this hunger for God's word.* – Derwin

We pass out tracts at our restaurant. Last night the following individual filled out the back and requested information and left it with our hostess. Please send your literature to him. – B.

I have just prayed to receive Jesus as my Savior. – Tom

Who Is
The American Tract Society?

A.T.S. is a nonprofit ministry dedicated to telling people the gospel or "good news" of Jesus Christ. The gospel is the good news that Jesus died for our sins (Romans 5:8). People become "believers" or Christians when they admit their sin to God, and then ask Jesus to be their Savior (John 3:16). In the biblical gospel account, Jesus took our place on the cross and rose again from the dead on the third day, proving that He was who He said He was. A.T.S. invites you to say a prayer right now to receive Jesus as your Lord. You have nothing to lose and only eternity in heaven to gain! This is our passion.

A Passion for People
For over 180 years, the American Tract Society (A.T.S.) has passionately followed Jesus' instructions to "go and make disciples of all nations." Billions of tracts, Bibles, and books have been published in over 188 different languages since 1825. With today's innovative technology in a postmodern world, A.T.S. continues to communicate God's relevant message of the gospel of Jesus Christ.

Our Mission
• To produce relevant and effective resources for evangelism
• To prepare and encourage Christians to present the gospel using those resources

Storied Tradition
Founded in New York City in 1825, A.T.S. was one of the earliest publishers of Christian literature in America. Its formation was a result of many different tract "societies" who wanted a national presence in a central location. A.T.S. can trace its development back to London in 1799 with the Religious Tract Society. Throughout pioneer America, A.T.S. distributed tracts, books and Bibles through a network of volunteers and "colporteurs." Some 600 to 800 of these traveling evangelists and workers visited over 21 million families with A.T.S. literature and conducted over 600,000 religious crusades or services. From the Tract Society's original "Statement of Purpose" in 1825—"To make Jesus Christ known in His redeeming Grace …"—comes our current vision: "Reaching the world with the life-changing gospel of Jesus Christ."

Powerful Tools
What is a "tract"? It is a focused, concise message centered on the gospel to move a person toward a decision for Christ. The message and images should resonate or literally grab the reader's attention. In today's world, you only have a few seconds to get someone's attention and then a minute to engage them in a conversation, or you'll lose them. A.T.S. tracts grab your attention and are easy to read, affordable, and true to the Scriptures. The stakes are high, the work is plentiful, and the need is urgent for evangelism in our world today. Amazingly, recent research reports that over half of all churchgoers cannot articulate the gospel. A.T.S. produces timely and relevant messages that help Christians tell others about Jesus Christ and

His gospel. Operation World tells us that over half of all evangelical Christians worldwide came to a saving knowledge of Christ, in part, through Christian literature like tracts. Tracts are effective because their messages travel farther, last longer, say it better, and cost less than any other means of evangelism.

Fast Food Evangelism Seminar

If you like what you've read in this book and want to implement any of these ideas in your church or Bible study group, we have good news for you. You can have an A.T.S. Certified *Fast Food* Trainer come to your location to present and discuss the theories and principles highlighted in this book!

In just two quick hours, this *Fast Food Evangelism Seminar* will cover all the important issues about sharing your faith with others.

Each seminar participant will receive:

- A copy of *Fast Food Evangelism*
- A *Fast Food Evangelism* interactive DVD
- Forty Gospel tracts
- Personal training with an A.T.S. Certified *Fast Food Evangelism* Trainer

We will also provide posters and materials to help you promote the *Fast Food Evangelism Seminar.*

For more information or to schedule a seminar, call 1-800-54-TRACT (548-7228) x 118 or email Evangelism@ATStracts.org

To learn more about the American Tract Society
or to see all our evangelistic tracts and resources,
visit us at www.atstracts.org